Animals, Tame and Wild

Program Authors

Connie Juel, Ph.D.

Jeanne R. Paratore, Ed.D.

Deborah Simmons, Ph.D.

Sharon Vaughn, Ph.D.

ISBN: 0-328-21426-4

PEARSON
Scott Foresman

1 2 3 4 5 6 7 8 9 10 V003 12 11 10 09 08 07 06

Editorial Offices: Glenview, Illinois • Parsippany, New Jersey • New York, New York
Sales Offices: Boston, Massachusetts • Duluth, Georgia • Glenview, Illinois
Coppell, Texas • Sacramento, California • Mesa, Arizona

Animals, Tame and Wild

Animal Friends

Wild Animals

Contents

Animal Friends

See page 19 for My New Words and Pictionary!

Let's Find Out

Taking Care of
PETS

I like the bird.

I like the cat.

I like the fish.

I like the dog.

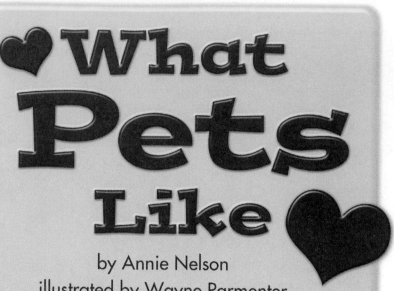

❤ What Pets Like ❤

by Annie Nelson

illustrated by Wayne Parmenter

The fish like the tank.

The kittens like the mouse.

The birds like the toy.

 The puppies like the towel.

Pets on a Mat

by Julian Cove • illustrated by Chris Lensch

I like the mat.

 I like the mat.

I like the mat.

 I like the mat.

WHICH IS A PET?

cat

turtle

moose

fish

turkey

dog

tiger

monkey

My New Words

I	**I** am in first grade.
like	I **like** puppies.
the	What is **the** name of your pet?

Pictionary

kitten

puppy

Contents

Animal Friends

See page 39 for My New Words and Pictionary!

People Help Animals

I am a vet.

I am a firefighter.

I am a dog walker.

I am a zookeeper.

Pam and Tam Tam

by Madison Wetzel
illustrated by Carolyn Croll

 Pam is a vet.

 Tam Tam is a puppy.

I look at Tam Tam.

I pat Tam Tam.

Tam Tam sat.

I like Tam Tam.

Sit, Sam!

by Percy Scott • illustrated by Ana Ochoa

I am Tim.

 Sam is a puppy.

Sit, Sam, sit.

Look at Sam sit.

I pat Sam.

Pat, pat, pat.

Sam pats Tim!

Old MacDonald Had a Farm

Old MacDonald had a farm, E–I–E–I–O.
And on his farm he had a dog, E–I–E–I–O.
With a "woof, woof" here,
And a "woof, woof" there,
Here a "woof," there a "woof,"
Everywhere a "woof, woof."
Old MacDonald had a farm, E–I–E–I–O!

2nd verse: cat   meow
3rd verse: cow   moo
4th verse: pig   oink

38

My New Words

a	Here is **a** pen.
is	**Is** he coming to your party?
	It **is** hot outside.
look	**Look** at the puppy.

Pictionary

firefighter

vet

Contents

Animal Friends

See page 59 for My New Words and Pictionary!

Animals Help People

Look at the camel.

Look at the cow.

Look at the sheep.

Look at the dog.

What We Like

by Grace Chin • illustrated by Christine Schneider

You have a chicken.

We like the eggs.

You have bees.

 We like the honey.

 You have a cow.

We like the milk.

You have a horse.

We like you.

BOB and TOM

by Jeb Wilson

illustrated by Guy Francis

I am Bob.

I am Tom.

We have a cab.

We like the cab.

We like you, Bob!
We like you, Tom!

Did You Know?

Dogs have good noses. They can smell much better than people. Dogs can sniff things out.

Dogs can find people who are lost.

Dogs can save people trapped in snow.

My New Words

have   I **have** a nickel in
             my pocket.

we   **We** are in the same class.

you   **You** can use my bike.

Pictionary

camel

honey

Contents

60

Wild Animals

See page 85 for My New Words and Pictionary!

See the Animals

Look at the seals.

Can you see the little seal?
Can you see its mom?

Look on top.

Monkeys are on top.

Look at the bears.

Can you see the little bear?
It naps.

See the little cat.

Its mom can not nap!

Little Cat

by David Lee

lion cub

See Little Cat.

lioness

lion

See its mom and dad.

Little Cat is tan.

Its mom and dad are tan.

Little Cat taps on its dad.

Its mom and dad sit.

Little Cat can nap.

Its mom and dad can nap.

The Ram Race

by Lin Tam • illustrated by Andy Elkerton

See little Dan Rat.
See little Nan Rat.

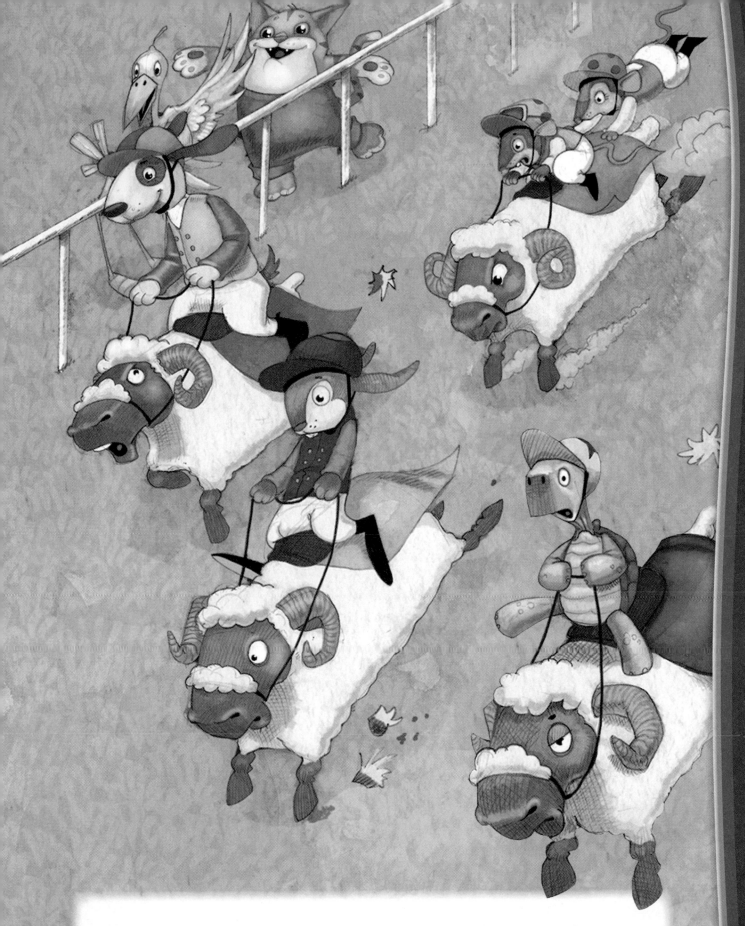

Dan and Nan are on Bob Ram.

Bob ran and ran.
Dan did not sit on Bob!

Nan did not sit on Bob.
Dan and Nan did not look!

Bob ran and ran.
Dan and Nan did look!

Dan and Nan pat Bob Ram.

What's for Dinner?

Read Together

This is a lion.
What does it eat?

This is a giraffe.
What does it eat?

This is a buffalo.
What does it eat?

This is a shark.
What does it eat?

Answers: Lions eat meat. Giraffes eat leaves and branches. Buffalo eat grass. Sharks eat other fish.

84

My New Words

are   Sam and Bob **are** ready.

little   A bee is **little**.

see   If you look in the box, you
          will **see** a toy.

Pictionary

nap

seal

Contents

Wild Animals

See page 117 for My New Words and Pictionary!

Animal Neighbors

Kass can see rabbits nap.

They nap in the tin pot.

Kip can see tan birds sip.

He can see tan birds go.

Kass and Kip can see a cob.

Squirrels nip at it.

Kass and Kip sit.

Kass and Kip can look.
Can you?

What Do They See?

by Alex Karpik • illustrated by Erika Le Barre

Biff can look at mountains.

Biff can see fat bears.

Don and Kim can go and look.

They can see fins.

Kit sits on sand.

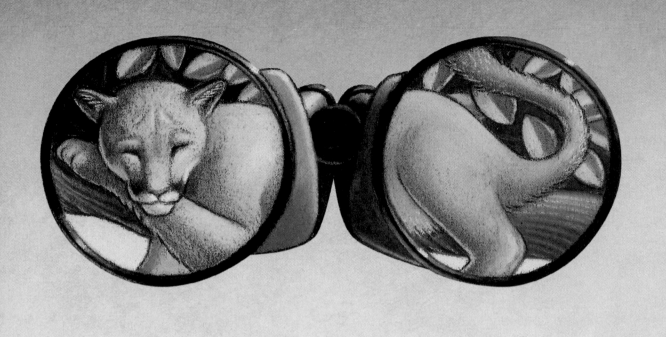

He can see a tan cat nap.

Cam can sit in a tree.

Cam can see deer.

Kep

by Rafael Cortez

illustrated by Jenny Harris

Kep is a fat, tan cat.

Kep can sit.
Kep can look.

Kep can see squirrels.

He can see red birds.

Kep ran at the red birds.
He can not go like birds.

Kep ran at the squirrels.
They ran and ran.

Can Kep nab birds?
Kep can not.

Can Kep nab squirrels?
Kep can not.

Look, Kep.

It is a mat.

Kep did not nab red birds.

Kep did not nab squirrels.

Kep did nab a nap.

Who Is Hiding?

Read each clue.
Find the hidden animals in the picture.

1. I eat nuts and have a bushy tail.

2. I have feathers.

3. I am green and croak.

4. I hop and like carrots.

My New Words

go   Are you ready to **go**?

he   **He** is my friend.

nab   If you **nab** something you grab and get it.

they   **They** are both my friends.

Pictionary

mountains

fin

Contents

Wild Animals

Animals Around the World

Ann hid in the hot sand.

She can see rabbits hop.
Hip, hop, hip, hop.

Ann can see ten animals.

Can you see ten?

Hap, Rob and Dad hid.

They can see frogs.

Do frogs hop on top of pads?
Hip, hop, hip, hop!

Dad, Hap, and Rob see ten animals.

Can you see ten?

At the Zoo

by Hunter Lobell

illustrated by Karen Lee Schmidt

Bill fed Hal.

Hal is a hippo.

Lin can mop an elephant.

She can mop at the tip top of it.

 Del let a zebra run in the pen.
It ran and ran and ran.

Bill, Lin, and Del do a lot.

Animals like Bill, Lin, and Del.

Nell Can Help

by Nikolas Alexander   illustrated by Liz Allen

 A sad whale is in mud and sand.

It can not go back in the water.

Nell can run.
She can run and tell.

A lot of men huff and puff.
They huff and puff in hot sun.

Can Nell do it too?

Nell can huff and puff.

The men and Nell can do it!

The whale is not in mud and sand.

The whale is back in the water.

Riddle Time

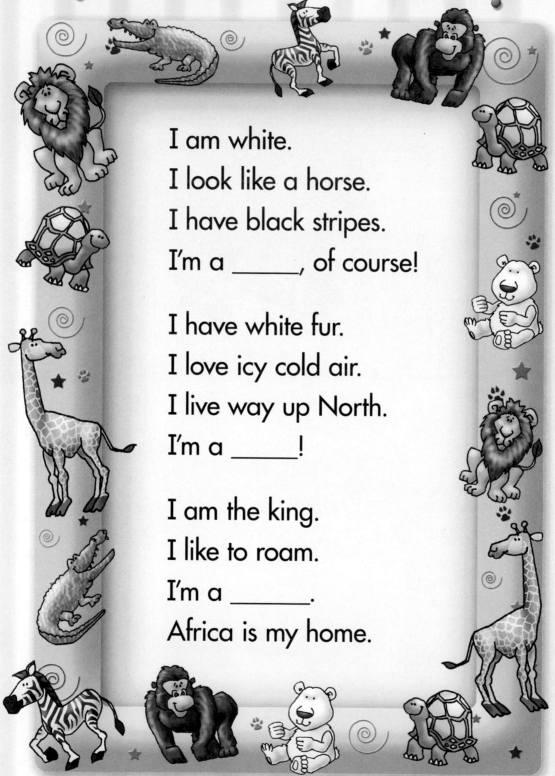

I am white.
I look like a horse.
I have black stripes.
I'm a _____, of course!

I have white fur.
I love icy cold air.
I live way up North.
I'm a _____!

I am the king.
I like to roam.
I'm a _____.
Africa is my home.

My New Words

do   Did you **do** your homework?

of   Here is a box **of** books.

she   My mother said **she** would drive.

Pictionary

animals

——pad

Acknowledgments

Illustrations

4, 14–17 Chris Lensch; **5, 18** Maggie Swanson; **10–13** Wayne Parmenter; **20, 32–37** Ana Ochoa; **21, 26–31** Carolyn Croll; **21, 38** Rose Mary Berlin; **40–41, 54–59** Guy Francis; **46–53, 59** Christine Schneider; **60, 78–83** Andy Elkerton; **61, 84** Steve Cox; **86, 104–114** Jennifer Beck Harris; **87, 96–103** Erika LeBarre; **87, 116, 118, 134–141** Elizabeth Allen; **88–94** Jason Wolff; **119, 128–133** Karen Lee Schmidt; **120–126** Kellie Lewis; **142** Don Tate.

Photographs

Every effort has been made to secure permission and provide appropriate credit for photographic material. The publisher deeply regrets any omission and pledges to correct errors called to its attention in subsequent editions.

Unless otherwise acknowledged, all photographs are the property of Scott Foresman, a division of Pearson Education.

Photo locators denoted as follows: Top (T), Center (C), Bottom (B), Left (L), Right (R), Background (Bkgd).

5 Getty Images; **6** (C, BR, TL, TC) Getty Images, (TR) ©Renee Lynn/Getty Images, (TC) Steve Shott/©DK Images; **7** (C) Aura/Getty Images, (BC) Getty Images; **8** (C) Comstock Images, (BC) Max Gibbs/ ©DK Images; **9** (C) ©Ariel Skelley/Corbis, (BR) Getty Images; **19** (BR, C) Getty Images; **22** (C) ©Ron Levine/Getty Images, (BC) ©Christopher Bissell/ Getty Images; **23** (C) ©Jochen Tack/Alamy Images, (BC) Getty Images; **24** (C) ©Kate Powers/Getty Images, (C) ©Paddy Ryan/Animals Animals/Earth Scenes, (BC) ©Royalty-Free/Corbis; **39** (BR) Getty Images, (BC) ©Christopher Bissell/Getty Images; **41** Getty Images; **42** (C) ©Dallas and John Heaton/ Stock Connection, (BC) ©GK Hart/Vikki Hart/Getty Images; **43** (C) Ron Redfern/©DK Images, (BC) ©Catherine Ledner/Getty Images; **44** (C) ©Nigel Cattlin/Photo Researchers, Inc., (BC) Getty Images, (BR) ©Alice Edward/Getty Images; **45** (BC) Getty Images, (C) ©Photofusion Picture Library/Alamy Images; **58** ©Mauro Fermariello/Photo Researchers, Inc.; **59** ©GK Hart/Vikki Hart/Getty Images; **61** ©Daryl Balfour/Getty Images; **62** (C, BC) Brand X Pictures; **63** Brand X Pictures; **64** ©Theo Allofs/Getty Images; **65** ©Theo Allofs/Getty Images; **66** (C, BC) Getty Images; **67** Getty Images; **68** ©Anup Shah/ Nature Picture Library; **70** ©Mike Hill/Alamy Images; **72** ©Daryl Balfour/Getty Images; **73** ©Angela Scott/Getty Images; **74** ©Art Wolfe/Getty Images; **75** ©Mitch Reardon/Getty Images; **76** ©Juniors Bildarchiv/Alamy Images; **77** Image Source/Getty Images; **85** (C, BR) Getty Images; **117** (C, BC) Getty Images; **143** (CL, C, BL) Getty Images.